GREAT
STAINED GLASS PROJECTS
for Beginners

GREAT
STAINED GLASS PROJECTS
for Beginners

SANDY ALLISON

Techniques demonstrated by Laird Morgan
Photographs by Alan Wycheck

STACKPOLE
BOOKS

Guilford, Connecticut

Published by Stackpole Books
An imprint of The Rowman & Littlefield
Publishing Group, Inc.
4501 Forbes Blvd., Ste. 200
Lanham, MD 20706
www.rowman.com

Distributed by
NATIONAL BOOK NETWORK
800-462-6420

Copyright © 2018 The Rowman & Littlefield
Publishing Group, Inc.

Photos by Alan Wycheck

Pattern designs by Laird Morgan unless
otherwise credited

British Library Cataloguing in Publication
Information available

**Library of Congress Cataloging-in-
Publication Data available**
ISBN 978-0-8117-3765-4 (paperback)
ISBN 978-0-8117-6744-6 (e-book)

♾™ The paper used in this publication meets
the minimum requirements of American
National Standard for Information Sciences—
Permanence of Paper for Printed Library
Materials, ANSI/NISO
Z39.48-1992.

Printed in the United States of America

CONTENTS

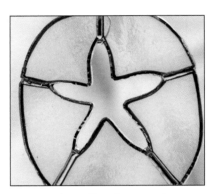

Sand Dollar Suncatcher
1

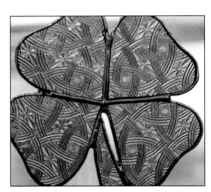

Lucky Shamrock
12

Falling Leaf
21

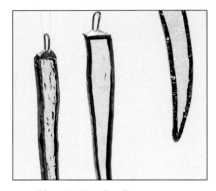

Classic Icicle Ornament
26

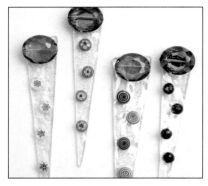

Icicle Ornament with
Bling **33**

Painted Snowman
Ornament **38**

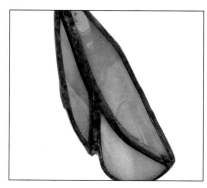

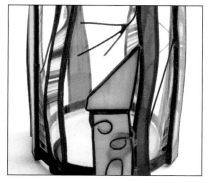
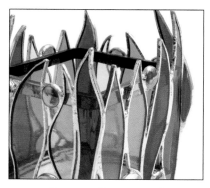

ABOUT THIS BOOK

YOU CAN MAKE strikingly beautiful and useful stained glass projects using simple basic techniques. This book offers instructions and step-by-step photographs, as well as full-size patterns, to show beginners how to make pendants, panels, holiday ornaments, candleholders, nightlights, and boxes, to name just a few. While the focus is on the projects and not on teaching basic skills, the first two projects here offer a quick review of all the basic techniques: using a pattern, selecting glass, scoring and cutting, grinding, foiling, soldering, and finishing. The material in the rest of the book will show you exactly how to handle the additional steps needed to create each of the great projects presented here.

We provide lists of materials each project requires beyond the basic tools. We also include general instructions about the glass used for each item. We decided not to offer specifics here—while the exact brand and style of glass used here might not be available at your local stained glass shop, it is sure to have something that will work just as well, if not better. Let the glass you see inspire you. There are so many styles and colors available.

The projects presented here can be interpreted in countless ways, with a multitude of different appearances and endless variations based on the glass you use.

Sand Dollar Suncatcher

A simple and beautiful reminder of the beach, to get you started.

Materials

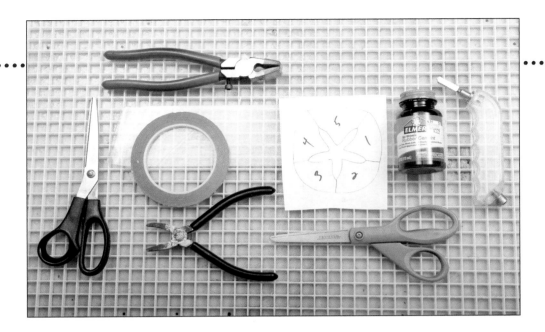

- Off-white glass
- 20-gauge tinned copper wire

1. Use pattern shears to cut apart the numbered pieces of the pattern.

2. Pattern shears remove a thin strip of paper between adjoining pieces to account for the width of the copper foil applied to the edges of the glass, otherwise the project wouldn't fit together properly when you're ready to solder.

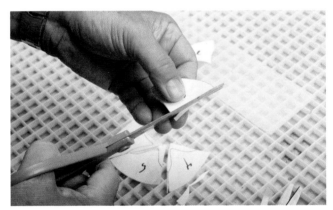

3. The edges of pieces that don't adjoin other pieces can be cut with standard scissors.

4. The pattern pieces are cut out and ready to go.

5. Apply rubber cement to the back of a pattern piece.

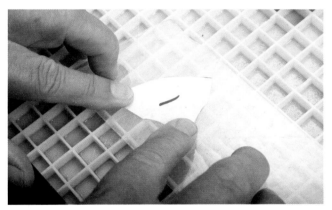

6. Attach the piece to the sheet of glass. Selecting the best portion of glass for the particular piece is something of an art. Taking time to choose carefully will make for a better finished product—especially if you're using streaked, wavy, or mottled glass.

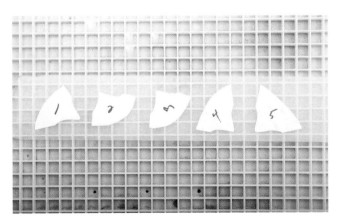

7. Attach each pattern piece to the glass.

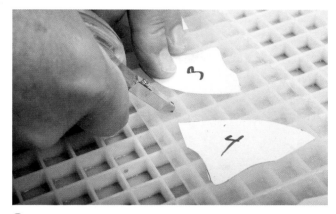

8. Score a straight line with the glass cutter between each piece.

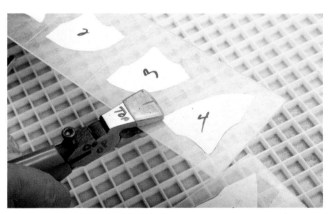

9. Use running pliers to separate the glass along the scored lines.

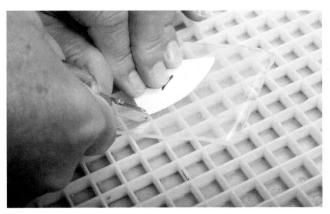

10. Score as close to the edge of the pattern paper as you can.

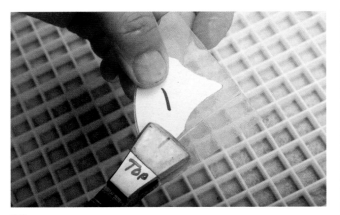

11. Use the running pliers to separate the glass along the scored lines.

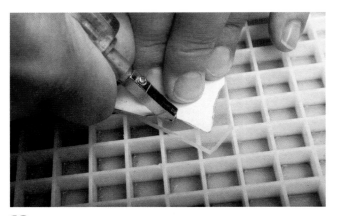

12. Small sections of glass require short scored lines.

13. Use grozing pliers to break off small pieces. Work carefully and be patient: Don't try to remove too much glass at once. Don't worry if the cut pieces have jagged edges or don't follow the pattern edges exactly.

TIP Don't forget proper technique when using running pliers. Make sure the flat upper jaw is on top of the glass. The jaw with the raised ridge should be on the bottom.

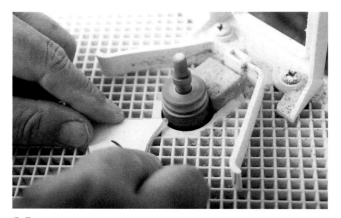

14. When each piece has been cut, use a grinder to remove excess glass and smooth the edges of the piece.

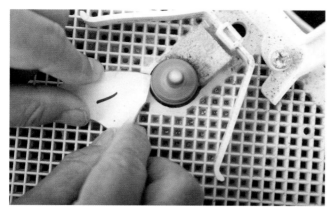

15. You'll be able to shape the pieces much more precisely with the grinder than you will with pliers.

18. It's wise to transfer the numbers from the pattern pieces to the glass so you know how to assemble the project.

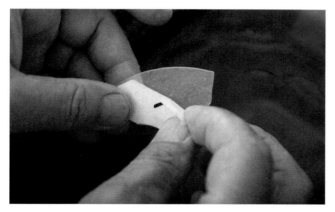

16. When you've finished grinding down all the pieces, remove the pattern paper from the glass.

19. A foiling machine makes applying copper foil to the edges of each piece much easier. But, of course, foiling can be done by hand.

17. All the edges should be smooth to the touch.

20. Apply foil in small sections. Don't try to foil the whole piece in one go.

21. Overlap the foil sections a bit, keeping the foil ends away from the glass corners.

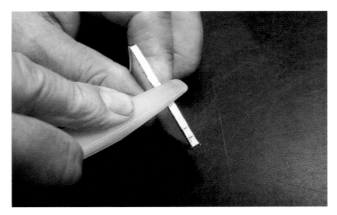

24. Use a plastic fid to rub the foil smooth. This helps it adhere tightly to the glass.

22. Press the foil down with your fingers so it adheres all around the glass edge.

25. Smooth the sides of the foil with the fid, too.

23. Foil the edges of each piece.

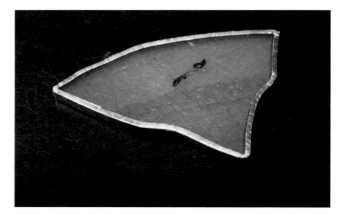

26. A well-foiled piece.

27. If the foil is slightly askew in places, don't pull it up and start over.

28. Use a sharp craft or utility knife to trim away the overlap.

29. Liquid flux is used here. Squirt a little into a plastic container.

30. Use a piece of sponge to apply flux to every part of the foil. Flux that comes in paste form applied with a brush works just as well.

31. When you have applied flux to every piece, assemble them to form the sand dollar.

32. Clean the hot soldering iron on a damp sponge.

33. The soldering iron temperature is right if a cooled bit of solder will melt and adhere when it is touched with the iron.

34. The first step in soldering is to tack the seams together.

35. Carefully tack each seam.

36. Then run a smooth bead of solder all along the tacked seams.

37. Apply a bit of solder to tin the top edges of the sand dollar.

38. Then tin the inside edges.

39. Make certain you cover every part of the foil. You don't want splotches of copper to show through.

40. The tinned edges should be smooth and consistent.

41. Flip the piece over and solder the other side.

42. A length of 20-gauge tinned copper wire is used to fashion a hanging hook for the project.

43. Bend the wire into a U shape using needle-nose pliers.

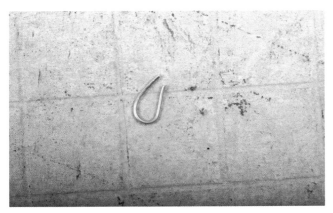

44. Trim off the U.

45. Apply flux to the wire, holding the small piece with the pliers.

46. Attach the wire to the back of the sand dollar on the seam you want to be at the top.

47. Use enough solder to attach the hook firmly.

48. The soldering is complete.

49. Clean off the flux and writing using a mild dishwashing liquid and water. A clean paintbrush will help.

50. Rinse the piece thoroughly with water. Stubborn pen marks can be removed with rubbing alcohol if necessary.

51. Dry the piece using a clean, soft towel.

52. Fishing line works well to hang the sand dollar invisibly. Pull it through the hook and tie it together.

Lucky Shamrock

Keep the luck of the Irish close at hand all throughout the year.

Materials

- Patterned kelly green glass
- 20-gauge tinned copper wire

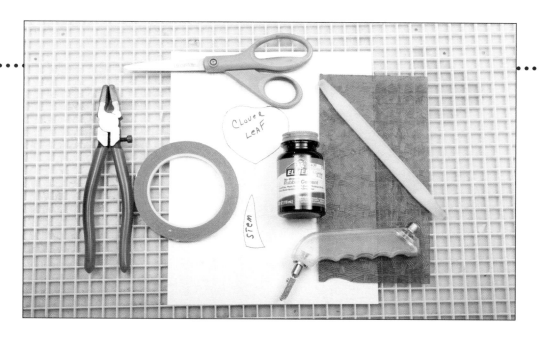

1. You can use regular scissors to cut apart these paper pattern pieces.

3. You can trace around the pattern pieces using a fine felt-tip marker, if you choose, or use rubber cement to attach the pieces to the glass.

2. The leaf piece will repeat four times.

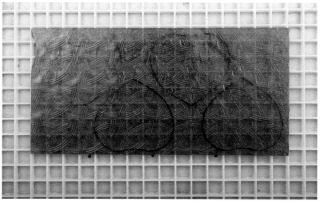

4. Two leaves were positioned upward and two downward so the glass pattern will alternate from leaf to leaf on the shamrock.

5. Don't forget to trace the stem.

6. Score the curves of one leaf.

7. Use running pliers to separate the glass.

8. Score the rest of the leaf piece.

9. Use grozing pliers to nibble away small pieces of glass.

10. Don't try to remove too much glass at one time. Be patient.

11. Grozing pliers are useful to cut out the stem, too.

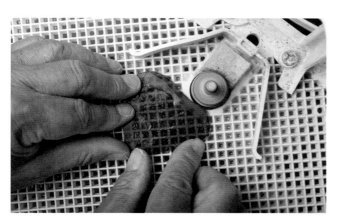

12. Smooth each piece using the grinder.

13. When the edges are smooth, foil the edges of each piece.

14. The leaves have only one corner and so foiling this project is a quick job.

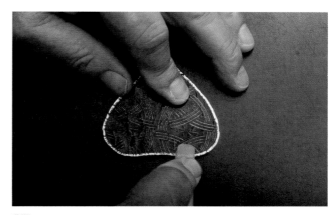

15. Use the fid to smooth the foil. This will help ensure the foil adheres tightly to the glass.

16. Because this glass has ridges, be extra careful that you've smoothed over every bit of the foil.

17. The foiled pieces are ready for soldering.

18. Apply flux to the foil.

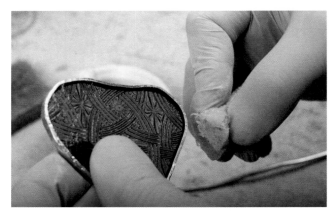

19. Don't skimp—better too much flux than not enough.

20. Begin soldering in the center of the shamrock to attach all four leaves together.

21. Attach the stem to the side of one leaf.

22. Run a line of solder along the seams where the pieces touch.

23. Work outward from the center.

24. All the seams are complete.

25. The next step is to tin the foil where it isn't touching another piece of glass.

26. Tin the outside of each leaf.

27. Work steadily around the curves.

28. When the top edge is tinned, do the sides.

29. Make sure the foil between the stem and the leaf is tinned so copper doesn't show through.

30. Turn the piece over.

31. Tin the backside of the shamrock.

32. Add solder to low spots if needed to help create a smooth bead.

33. You can clean up rough spots with a quick touch of the iron.

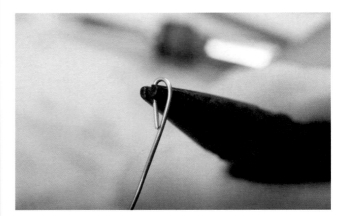

34. To create a hanging hook, bend a piece of 20-gauge wire using needle-nose pliers.

35. Trim off the U shape to make the hook.

36. Apply flux to the hook.

37. Solder it where two leaves meet.

38. Attach the hook firmly. A little tug when the solder is cool will tell you if the hook will hold.

39. Carefully bend the hook upward if it's too flat.

40. Attach a second hook as shown so the shamrock will hang straight.

41. Clean the piece with dish soap and a soft brush.

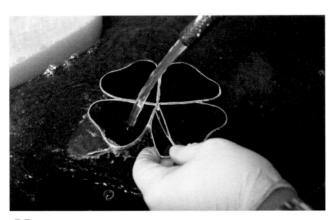

42. Rinse the piece.

43. Dry it gently with a soft towel.

Falling Leaf

Make leaves in a variety of colors: subtle shades of fall, or fresh shades of spring.

Materials

- Streaky autumn orange glass
- Streaky springtime green glass
- 20-gauge tinned copper wire

1. The eight paper pattern pieces were carefully positioned on the streaky glass so that the finished piece will have the desired color pattern. Look closely and envision how each piece will appear within the whole. Let the glass inspire you.

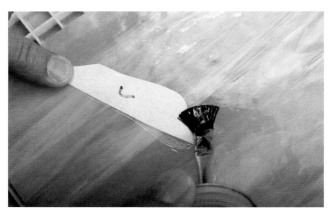

2. When the placement is decided, each pattern piece is glued to the glass.

3. Cut away unused glass to use for a future project.

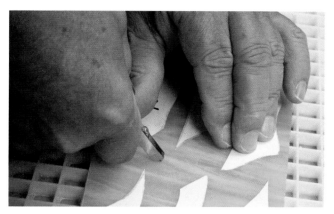

4. Score carefully. This streaky glass has bumps and ridges that make cutting a bit tricky.

5. Working patiently will give you the best results.

6. Running pliers can be used effectively on even small pieces of glass.

7. Pattern shears were used to cut apart the paper pattern. The green streaky glass will make a beautiful springtime leaf.

8. For this leaf, the pattern pieces were positioned so that the streaks would flow across the adjacent pieces of the leaf's three sections.

9. When the position is established, glue the pieces down.

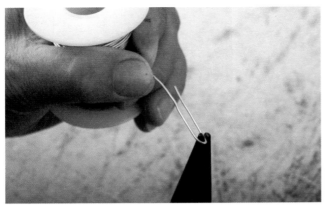

10. After the project has been foiled and soldered together, 20-gauge wire is used to make a stem. Twist the wire into a long U.

11. Use needle-nose pliers to grab the U's open end. Then turn the plier to twist the wire. Keep a small opening in the tip.

12. Make three or four twists. The stem should be about 1½ inches long.

13. Position the wire on the back of the leaf to form a stem. Apply flux.

14. Solder the stem firmly in place.

15. Smooth out any lumps with a touch of the iron.

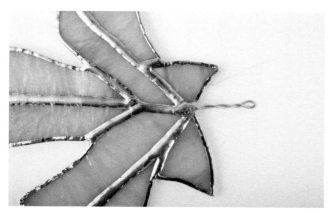

TIP It's best to stay away from ribbons or string when hanging pieces. Stained glass projects can be heavy. Use plastic fishing line or chains of substantial twine to prevent accidents.

16. String fishing line through the stem loop and tie it together to make a hanger.

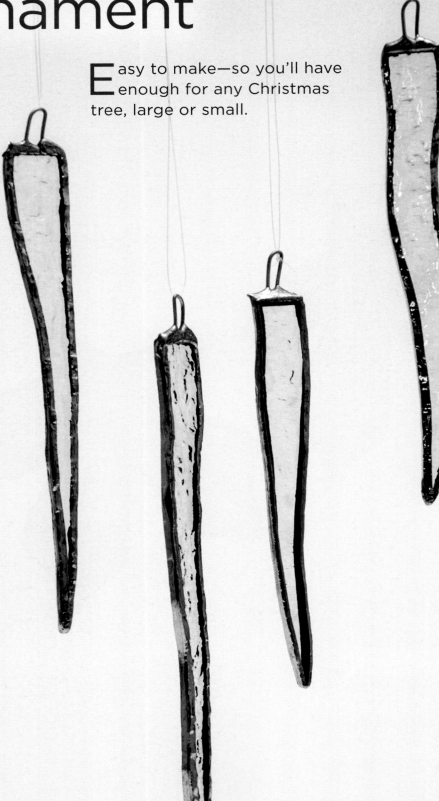

Classic Icicle Ornament

E asy to make—so you'll have enough for any Christmas tree, large or small.

Materials

- Shimmery silver-white glass
- 20-gauge tinned copper wire
- Fishing line or colored ribbon to hang

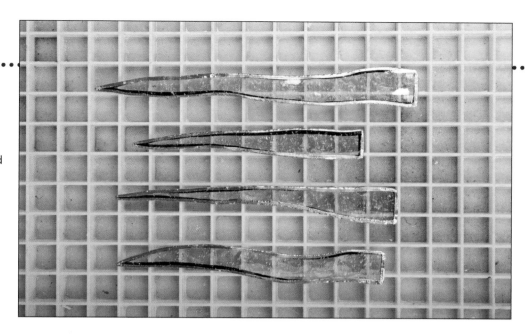

1. Foiling and tinning the edges of these ornaments gives them a finished look and provides a place to attach the hanging hook.

3. Foiling at the tip is the trickiest part. Be careful that the point doesn't poke through the foil.

2. Press the foiled edges down carefully on the crinkly glass.

4. Use a fid to smooth the foil.

5. Work carefully to avoid tearing or dislodging the foil.

6. Apply flux to the foiled piece.

TIP Some brands of flux are made to emit less smoke and fewer fumes than other brands. Check the label before you buy.

7. Tin each piece to cover the copper.

8. Do the front first.

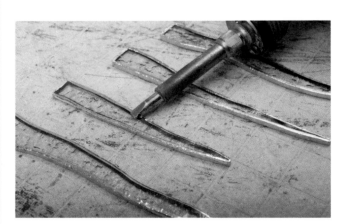

9. Make sure no foil shows through.

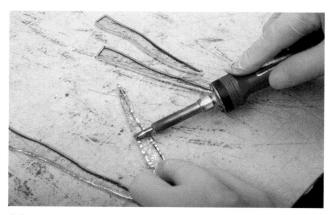

10. Tin the sides and the backs of each ornament.

11. To make a hook for the icicles, bend 20-gauge wire into a flattened loop, as shown.

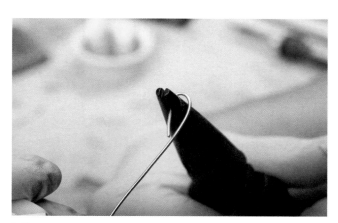

12. Bend the wire until the tip almost touches the wire.

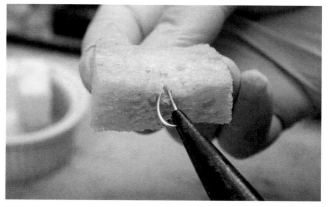

13. Cut the loop off and apply flux.

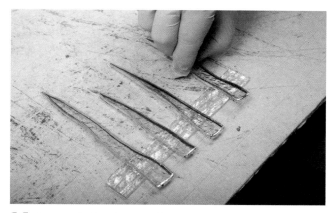

14. To apply hooks to a few ornaments at one time, set them on a length of scrap glass to lift the ends off the work surface.

15. Tape the pieces down with masking tape to hold them in place as you solder.

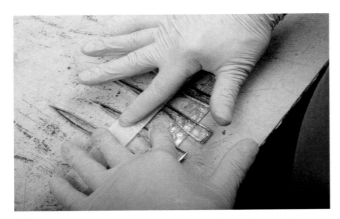

16. Make sure the tape sticks to the surface of each piece.

17. The hook will be soldered with the ends on either side of the icicle.

18. Hold the hook in place with needle-nose pliers and apply flux.

19. Make sure to flux both sides of the loop.

20. Solder the loop firmly in place.

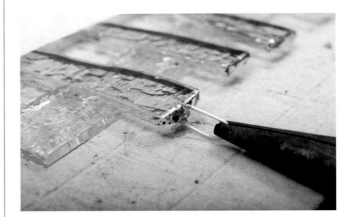

21. Make sure the soldering holds.

22. An alternate way of making a hook is to bend the wire into a loop "with shoulders."

23. Trim the piece so each shoulder is the same length.

24. The piece should be just as wide as the top of an icicle.

25. Hold the piece against the icicle and apply flux. Note that it's easier to solder these hooks if the icicles are not propped up and taped down as before.

26. Solder each shoulder to the icicle.

TIP Soldering irons can vary—don't assume that the same setting will make every iron as hot as others. It's best to test any iron you use on scrap glass before starting a project.

27. Make sure the solder holds.

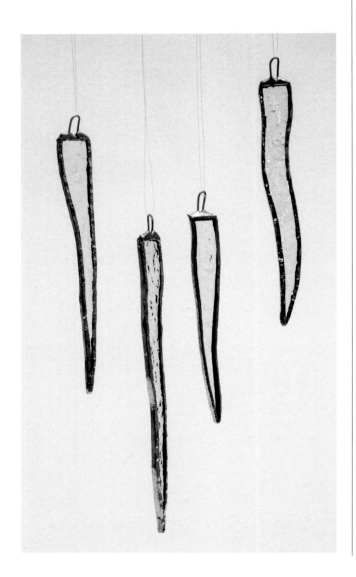

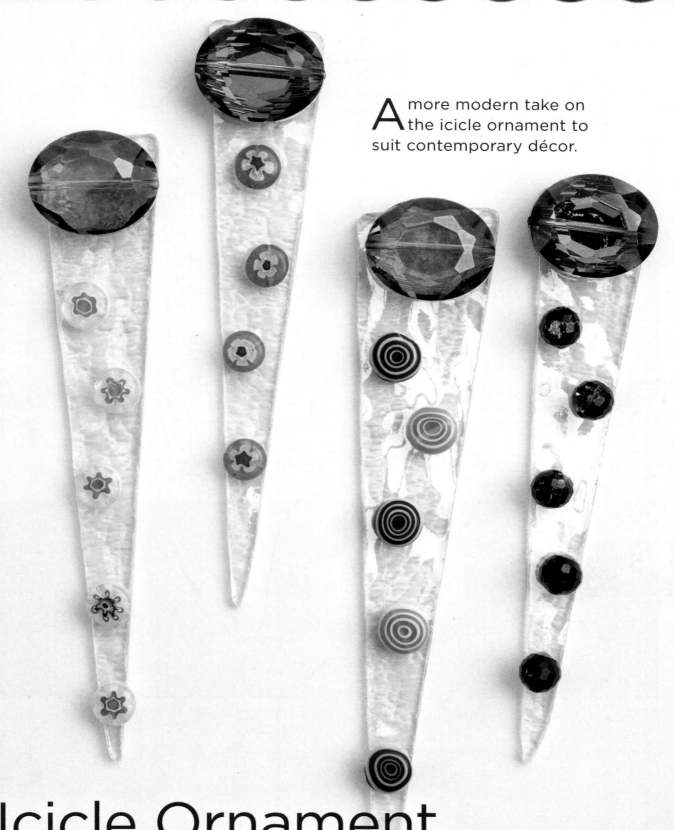

A more modern take on the icicle ornament to suit contemporary décor.

Icicle Ornament
with Bling

Materials

- Iridescent white glass
- Swirled glass buttons
- Glass nuggets with a hole
- Adhesive suitable for glass
- 20-gauge tinned copper wire
- Fishing line or colored ribbon to hang

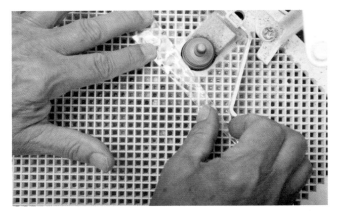

1. Smooth the edges of these icicles using the grinder, even though they won't be foiled.

3. Work carefully so the edges remain straight. If you hold the piece against the grinding wheel in one spot for too long you'll create a small indention.

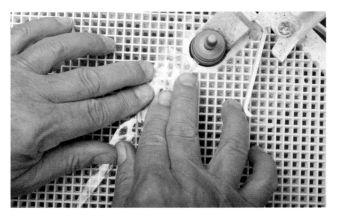

2. Make sure all jagged or sharp edges are smoothed off.

4. The icicles are shaped and smooth and ready for the next step.

5. Swirled glass buttons are available in stained glass shops or craft stores. Or you can scour flea markets and antique malls for pieces.

6. Large glass nuggets or jewels with holes through them will be used at the top of each icicle.

7. Costume jewelry pieces can be a great source of glass beads.

8. An adhesive such as Goop will work well on glass. Read the label carefully to make sure what you use will hold glass together securely.

9. Apply a generous dollop of adhesive to the back of a large nugget.

10. Press it into place at the top of the icicle. Keep pressing until the glue sets per the instructions on the label.

11. Sort out the smaller buttons you want for the rest of the icicle.

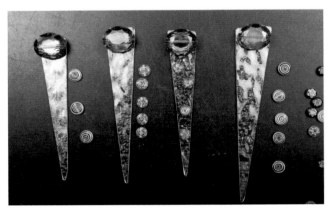

12. Arrange the smaller pieces to suit. Remember: There really is no incorrect way to arrange your pieces of bling.

13. Glue the buttons in place using a smaller amount of adhesive.

14. You don't want excess adhesive oozing out when the piece is attached.

15. Press the pieces in place until the adhesive sets.

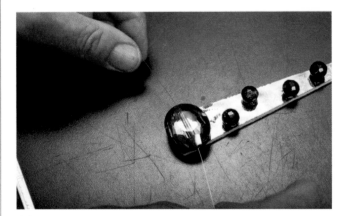

16. Run a piece of fishing line through the large bead to serve as a hanger. A thin strip of ribbon in a coordinating color would work, too.

17. Tie the line together to finish the ornament.

TIP Of course, you can use any sort of bead you want on this project. Coordinate your holiday décor by selecting colors and styles that match your other tree decorations.

Painted Snowman Ornament

Hand painting the face and customizing the arms make each snowman one of a kind.

Materials

- Snow-white glass
- Glass in two complementary colors (for the hat)
- Glass paint and fine brush
- 20-gauge tinned copper wire
- Fishing line or colored ribbon to hang

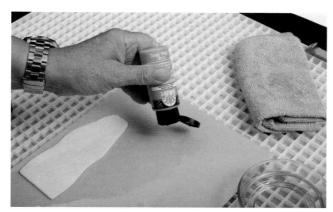

1. Squeeze a small amount of paint onto a palette—a spare piece of glass will work for this. You can clean off the excess paint before it dries and still use the glass for another project.

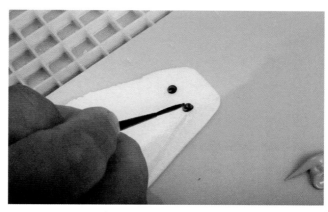

3. Make sure the snowman is clean and dry before applying the paint.

2. Wet the brush with clean water and mix a little into the paint to thin it a bit.

4. Paint your snowman's face however you wish. The glass paint used here is hardened by heating the painted glass in the oven at 300 degrees for 30 minutes.

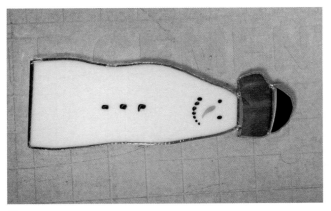

5. Apply foil to the snowman and the hat. Then tin the snowman and solder the hat to his head.

6. Use 20-gauge wire for the arms. Establish the length you want.

7. And trim the wire.

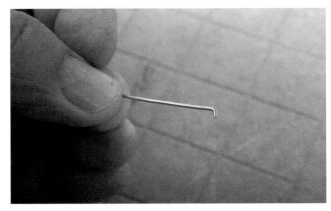

8. Bend the wire tip to form a 90-degree angle.

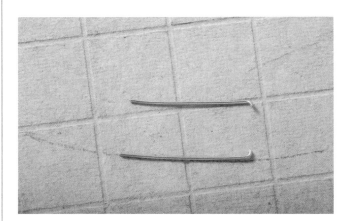

9. Repeat for the other arm.

TIP Pliers made for beaded jewelry are very useful if you bend a good amount of wire. Look for ones with rounded jaws that make round shapes easily and quickly.

10. Bend wire into a wide V shape to create a hand and trim off the V. Make two Vs.

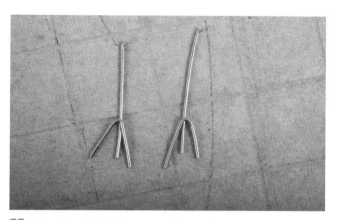

11. The Vs will help you make perfect snowman hands.

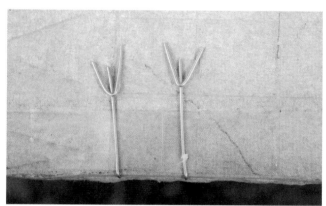

12. To attach the Vs, tape the arms to hold them in place.

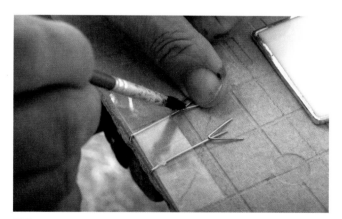

13. Lay the Vs on top of the wire arms and apply flux.

14. Solder the hands together. Placing a cutting tool or other implement as shown to act as a brace will help you keep the Vs from sliding forward.

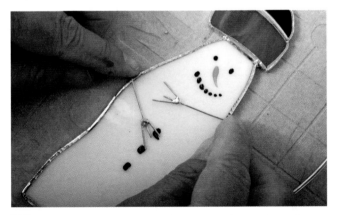

15. Arrange the arms, making sure the end angles overlap the snowman's sides.

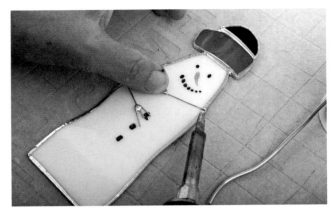

16. Flux and solder the arms in place.

17. Gently bend the arms with pliers to give them elbows.

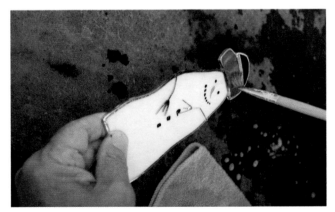

18. A patina was applied to darken this snowman's foil. Clean the piece thoroughly after applying the patina.

19. Be careful when you rinse off the little guy. To create a hanger, solder a hook to the top of the hat, or glue a hook to the back using Goop adhesive.

TIP There are a number of different paints available that are suitable for glass. Many require heating in an oven to set them. Refer to the instructions for proper heating temperatures and times. You can also find glass paint markers in craft stores and online. These make adding decoration to stained glass projects an easy task.

Tiny Leaf Pendant

Atiny little leaf using handmade glass makes a distinctive pendant.

Materials

- Handmade mottled green glass
- Lead-free solder
- 20-gauge tinned copper wire
- Chain at desired length

1. This pretty little piece makes use of handmade glass with a mottled green pattern. Look for the perfect section of glass to show on your pendant. Cut, grind, and foil the piece.

3. Then draw four small lines out to the leaf's points.

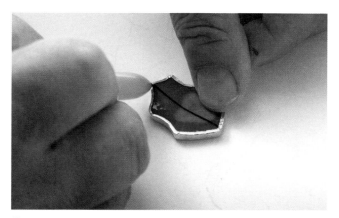

2. To mark out the pattern for the leaf veins, use a felt tip marker with a fine point. Draw a line from tip to stem.

4. Lay a piece of 20-gauge wire along the centerline to determine the proper length.

5. Bend the tip using needle-nose pliers to form a slight crook.

6. Lay the piece on the glass with the crook overlapping the tip, as shown. Mark the other end about ⅛ inch past the pendant.

7. Cut the wire at the mark.

8. Bend the wire to form another crook in the same direction as the first one.

9. Bend only about ⅛ inch.

10. The wire should slip onto the pendant. Hold it in place with pliers.

11. Apply flux to the end of the wire.

12. Lead-free solder is used for this pendant. It will prevent the piece from causing irritation if worn against the skin. It's wise to use lead-free solder for any jewelry. In general, the techniques for lead-free solder are the same as for standard lead solder.

13. Solder one end of the wire to tack it in place.

14. Make sure the other end fits in place.

15. Apply flux.

16. Tack it in place.

17. Make sure the wire is attached firmly. You can always touch up the solder to smooth it down.

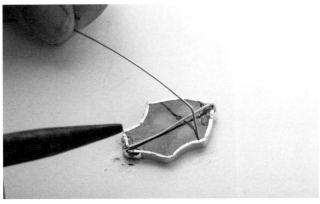

18. Now measure out the proper length for the cross pieces. It's helpful to bend the wire in its middle very slightly to create a tiny hump.

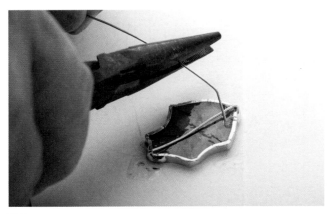

19. Mark the wire, then trim it. There's no need to create overhangs for the cross pieces.

20. Hold the wire in place and apply flux.

21. Do both sides.

22. Tack one end in place.

23. Make sure it holds.

24. Hold the other end in place with the pliers.

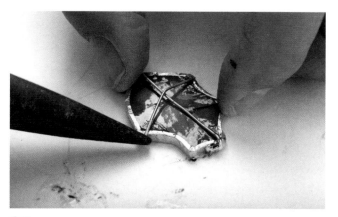

25. Trim off any overhang if necessary.

26. Solder the other end in place.

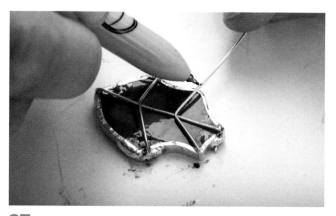

27. Attach the second cross piece in the same way.

TIP Keeping the tip of your soldering iron clean is the key to good soldering. Use a wet sponge to clean the tip. Or buy a block of sal ammoniac (available from stained glass suppliers), which effectively removes carbon buildup.

28. It might require some fiddling and trimming to get the wire positioned and attached the way you want it to be.

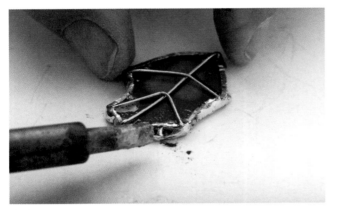

29. Tin the sides of the pendant, smoothing out any blobs as you go.

30. Cover the foil all around the pendant.

31. Flux and solder the spots where the wires touch.

32. The wires should all hold firmly.

33. Don't forget to tin the foil on the back of the pendant.

34. Fashion a hook for the pendant using 20-gauge wire.

35. Flux the ends of the hook.

36. Solder it in place.

37. Wash the pendant thoroughly to remove all the markings and flux.

38. Dry with a soft cloth to make the pendant shine.

Tiny Feather Pendant

W ear this charm around your neck as a beautiful and unique conversation starter.

Materials

- Iridescent glass in three different shades
- 20-gauge tinned copper wire
- Aged copper patina
- Chain at desired length

1. Cut, grind, and foil these tiny slivers of beautiful iridescent glass.

2. Flux all the edges.

3. Solder where foil touches foil first. As with any jewelry, it's best to use lead-free solder for this project.

4. Then tin the edges.

5. Touch up the solder if needed to create a smooth line.

6. Hold the piece in place using needle-nose pliers.

7. When the front and sides are complete, solder the back of the pendant.

8. Work carefully to cover all the foil.

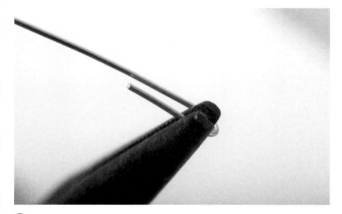

9. Bend the tip of 20-gauge wire to form a deep U shape.

10. Trim the U, hold it in place on the pendant, and apply flux.

11. Solder the hook in place.

12. Give it a tug to make sure it's secure.

13. Wash the piece with dish soap.

14. Rinse it completely.

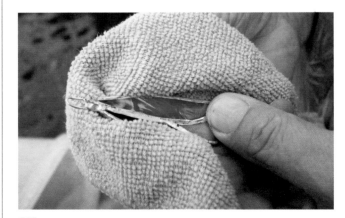

15. Dry it carefully with a soft cloth.

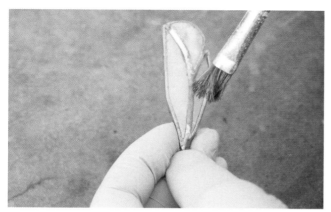

16. A patina is applied to the solder of the feather pendant using a paintbrush. It will give the silver solder the look of aged copper. Be sure to wear rubber gloves when you work with patina.

17. The patina will begin to change the color of the solder after a few seconds.

18. Apply patina to every part of solder, then wash the piece thoroughly with soapy water.

19. Rinse to remove all the patina.

Large Feather Suncatcher

A larger feather to hang in a sunny window, or display anywhere.

Materials

- Iridescent glass in any shade
- 20-gauge tinned copper wire

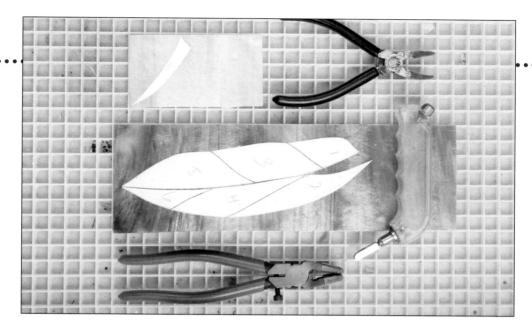

1. As with the Falling Leaf project, the pattern pieces for the large feather are arranged so that the streaks in the glass extend from one piece into the adjoining one.

3. Break the glass in half using running pliers.

2. Score the centerline of the feather.

4. Score along a diagonal line.

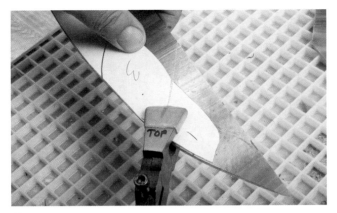

5. Break off the sections one by one.

6. Careful scoring and breaking means no cracked glass—if you're lucky.

TIP If you do a lot of stained glass making, it's wise to invest in a quality grinder. A good tool will make it much easier to shape cut glass precisely and quickly. Don't skimp.

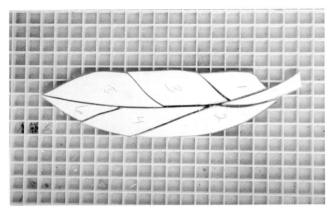

7. When assembled, the feather will look as though it's made of a single piece of glass.

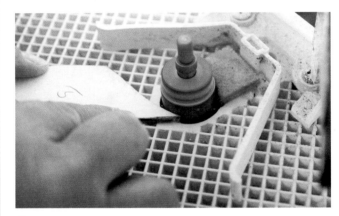

8. Grind carefully.

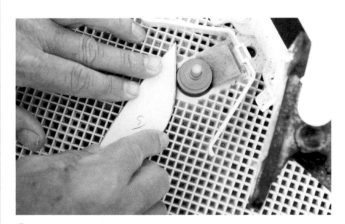

9. Maintain the points on the glass pieces.

10. Solder the piece and attach a hanging hook as with previous projects.

Round Decorated Candleholder

Transform a plain glass container into a contemporary work of art.

Materials

- Round clear glass container
- Streaky red and red glass
- Glass in two complementary colors for the two-piece element
- 20-gauge tinned copper wire
- ⅜-inch-wide copper foil

1. Use ⅜-inch-wide copper foil for this project. Cut off a piece that will wrap all the way around the outside edge of the top of the glass container.

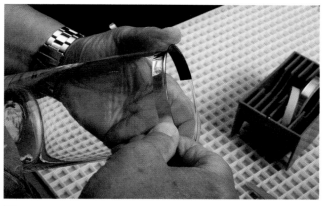

3. Make sure the foil is smooth and fastened securely to the glass.

2. Apply the foil to the edge as shown. Trim the end to create a slight overlap. It's better to do this than have a gap between the ends.

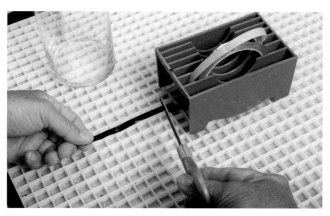

4. Cut another strip of foil for the bottom of the container.

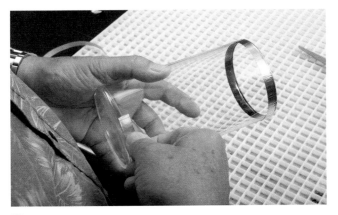

5. Apply it to the outside bottom edge.

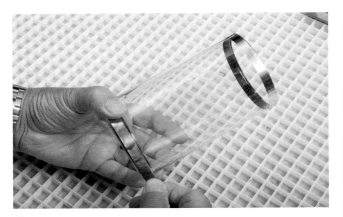

6. Make sure it's secure, then trim the end.

7. Smooth the foil using a fid. The copper should be smooth and shiny.

8. Use the edge of the fid to make the edge seam tight.

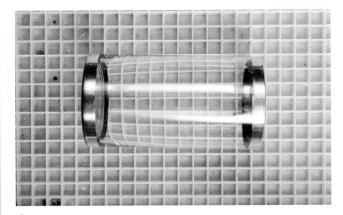

9. The foil has been applied and smoothed out.

10. Apply flux to the foil of the stained glass pieces. If you plan to do all the tinning in one go, you can flux all the pieces.

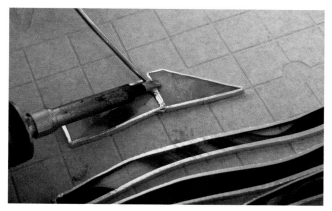

11. Solder the two-piece decorative element together and tin the edges before attaching it to the candleholder.

14. Apply flux to the wide foil on the container.

12. Tin the sides of all the side decorations.

15. Tin the wide foil, both top and bottom.

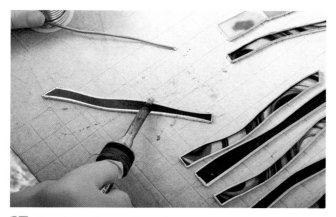

13. Do the sides and the back of all the pieces.

16. Lay one of the side pieces along the container as shown, making sure the flat edge doesn't extend beyond the container's base.

17. Solder both sides of the top and bottom ends of the stained glass strip to attach it to the container.

18. Use enough solder so the piece is firmly attached.

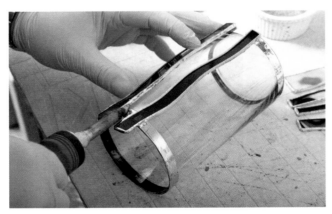

19. Attach the other side pieces. This glass container has a circumference of 11 inches and is 6 inches high. The side pieces are spaced about ¾ inch apart. You'll need to plan out the spacing on your container before you solder if it is larger or smaller.

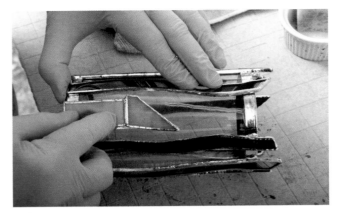

20. The gap is filled in with the two-piece element.

21. It's soldered at the bottom and at the top to a side piece as shown.

22. Draw curls on the two-piece element.

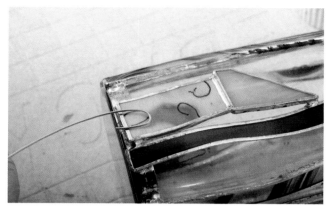

23. Bend 20-gauge wire to match the drawn curls.

24. Set the trimmed wire curls in place and apply flux.

25. Use the tip of needle-nose pliers to hold the wire as you solder the wire in place.

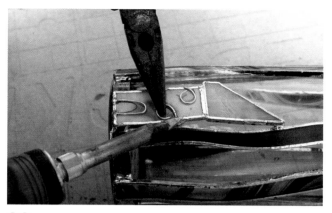

26. This work is a bit fiddly. Be patient.

27. The decorative wire swirls in between the side pieces are bent, cut, and soldered in place in the same way.

28. Use your imagination to create the swirls however you wish.

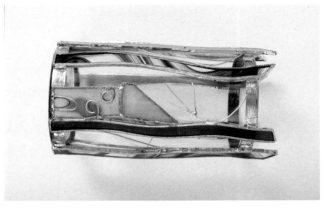

29. All the wire elements should be firmly attached so they don't pop off.

30. Wash the piece with dish soap using a clean brush.

31. Rinse carefully.

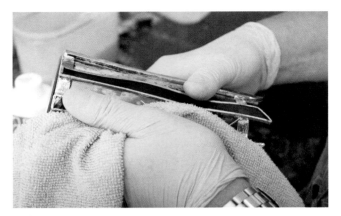

32. Dry the piece.

33. Black patina is used to darken the silver solder. To apply the patina, first pour a small amount into a clean plastic container. Don't forget to wear rubber gloves.

34. Brush the patina over every silver surface.

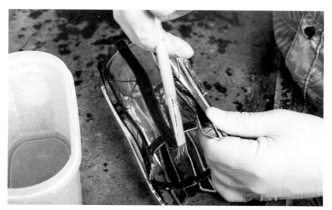

35. Make sure you hit every spot. The silver will darken after a few seconds and you'll be able to see if you missed a spot.

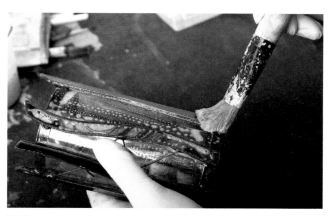

36. Use soapy water to remove excess patina.

38. A final dry and shine will complete the piece.

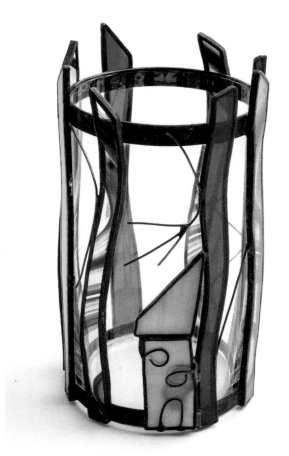

37. Rinse the piece completely.

Square Decorated Candleholder

A variation of the round candleholder using the same techniques.

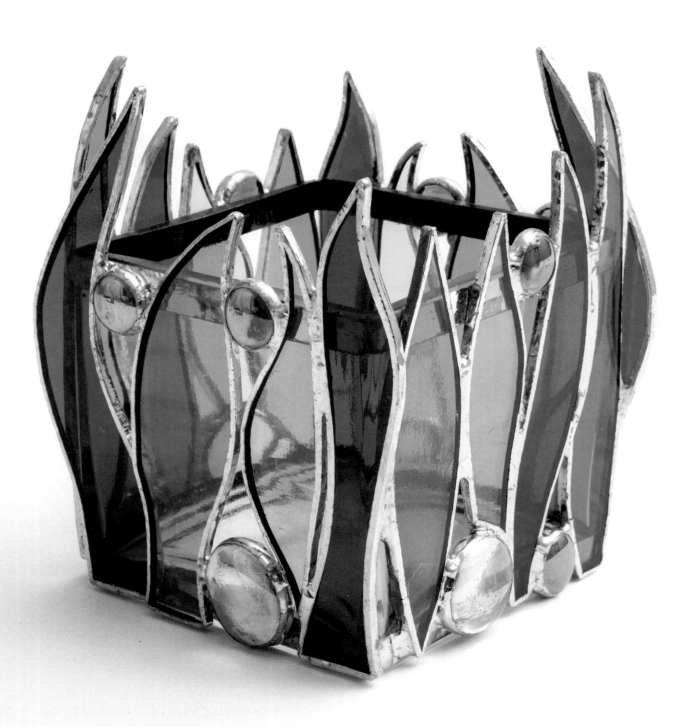

Materials

- Square clear glass container
- Red, orange, and yellow glass
- Glass nuggets in complementary colors
- 20-gauge tinned copper wire
- ⅜-inch-wide copper foil

1. Apply a strip of ⅜-inch-wide copper foil to the top of the container.

3. It's best if the foil wraps around the corners a bit. Wrap the bottom of the container the same way.

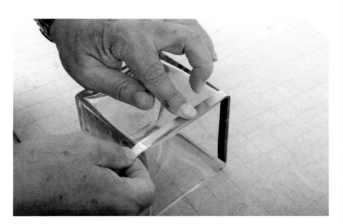

2. Press it down so it adheres completely.

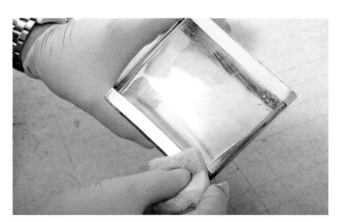

4. Apply flux to both the foil strips.

5. Flux the foiled beads as well.

6. Flux and tin the decorative side pieces before you attach them to the container.

7. Tin the foiled nuggets, too.

8. Then tin the foil on the container, top and bottom.

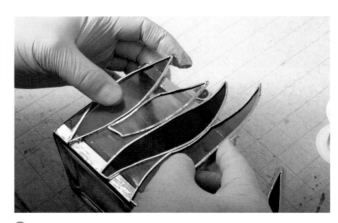

9. Arrange the side pieces on one side of the container, making sure they don't extend beyond the container's bottom.

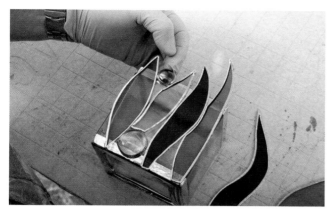

10. The beads will fit above and below the shorter side piece.

13. Run a line of solder along the seams.

11. When you're satisfied with the arrangement, it's time to solder.

14. Make sure the sides of the pieces are tacked, too.

12. Tack the pieces to the container, then tack them together where they touch. Tack the nuggets to the container and side pieces as well.

15. Soldering wherever the pieces touch will keep them from wobbling.

16. Complete the rest of the container the same way.

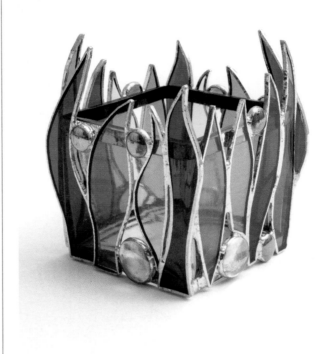

Potted Flowers

These pretty potted flowers will stay bright and colorful all year.

Materials

- Carnation red glass
- Bluebell blue glass
- Bright green glass
- Terra cotta-colored glass
- Foam stained glass support blocks

Pattern by Nancy Wiswell, Ladybug Stained Glass

1. The trickiest part of making the potted flowers is applying the triangular side support pieces. The first step is to apply flux to the foil.

3. Foam support blocks made especially for stained glass projects are used to prop up the flowers so the side pieces can be attached. These blocks won't burn if hot solder is dropped on them.

2. Then tin the pieces, front, back, and sides.

4. The flower should lean at the same angle as the short side of the side piece.

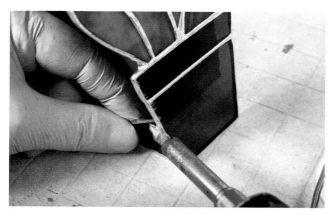

5. Tack the piece in place.

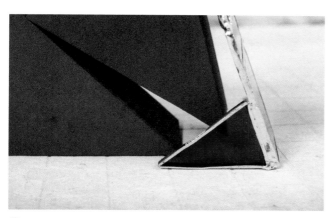

6. The solder should hold firmly.

7. Attach the other side support the same way.

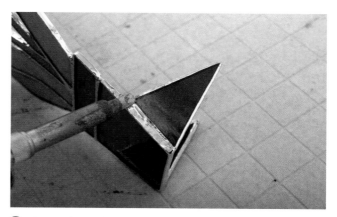

8. Run a line of solder all along the seam on both sides.

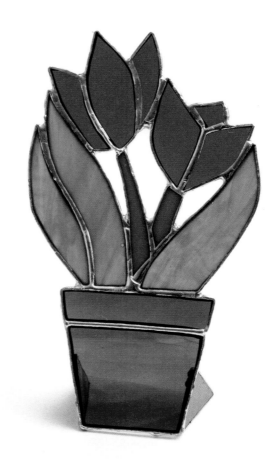

9. Then tack the bottom of the side piece where it meets the flowerpot's bottom edge.

Pineapple
Nightlight

A warm and welcoming nightlight provides a soft glow wherever you need it.

Materials

- Pineapple yellow glass
- Green glass
- 20-gauge tinned copper wire
- Nightlight fixture and bulb
- Adhesive for glass

1. The zigzag design on the face of the pineapple is made from lengths of 20-gauge wire.

3. Trim the wire.

2. Measure a length from the bottom right (5 o'clock) of the pineapple to the left side (between 8 and 9 o'clock).

4. Set it on the pineapple.

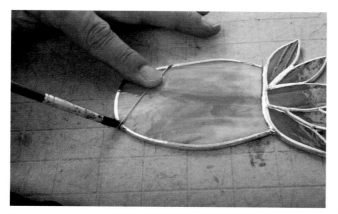

5. Flux the ends.

6. And solder it in place.

7. Work your way diagonally up the pineapple in the same way.

8. Use the tip of your pliers to gently nudge the wires into position.

9. Then add the cross pieces, trimming, fluxing, and soldering them into place.

10. There's no need to solder the wires where they touch (unless you want to).

11. Clean the piece thoroughly.

12. Make sure it's dry.

13. Goop adhesive will be used to attach the light fixture to the back of the piece.

14. Apply a generous amount of glue to the fixture's clip.

15. Press it into place. Let it set up according to the directions on the tube.

16. When the adhesive is dry, clip the fixture into place.

17. Use the screw to tighten the clip.

Dragonfly Garden Stake

This fun and distinctive decoration is perfect for the garden or a large potted plant.

Materials

- Shimmering silvery glass
- Dark green glass
- Round green glass nugget
- 20-gauge tinned copper wire
- ⅛-inch brass rod about 26 inches long

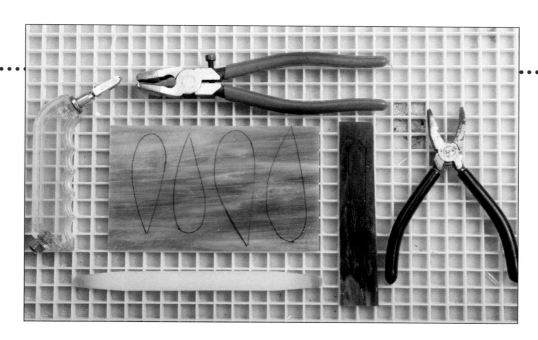

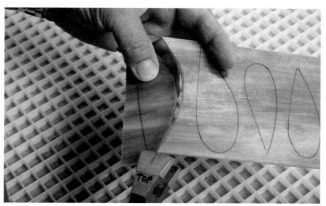

1. Cut out the four wings. Curves are trickier than straight pieces; you'll want to score and break small pieces with this project.

3. The straight body piece is easier to cut.

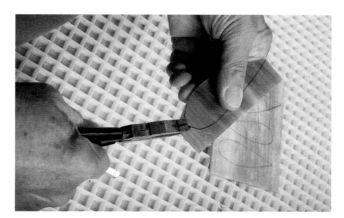

2. The grozing pliers will come in handy to nibble away at the curves.

4. All that's needed now is the head.

5. Tin and solder the dragonfly together.

6. Then lay a length of ⅛-inch brass rod on the back of the dragonfly, as shown. A 26-inch length of tubing is used here. Flux the rod where it overlaps the dragonfly.

7. Then tin the rod.

8. Cover as much as will be in contact with the dragonfly.

9. Then tack the rod to the dragonfly's back.

10. Use a fair amount of solder so the attachment is secure.

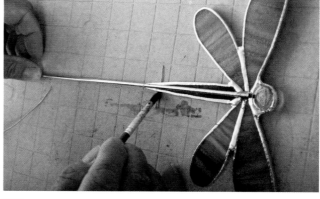

13. Flux it where it touches the solder.

11. Next trim off a 2-inch piece of 20-gauge wire. This will form a support wrap around the dragonfly's tail.

14. Solder to attach it.

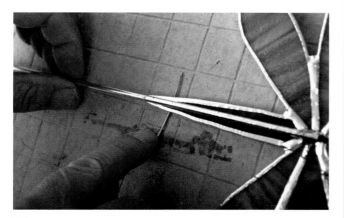

12. Set the bottom of the dragonfly on the wire.

15. Pull up the ends of the wire with needle-nose pliers.

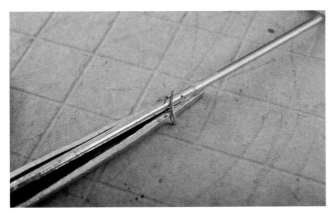

16. Wrap them around the rod. Trim off any excess.

18. Flux and solder the ends to make the wrap secure.

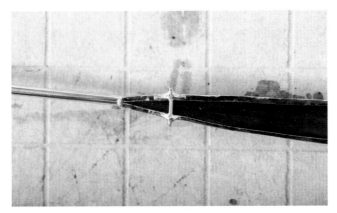

17. The ends of the wire should touch each other and the rod.

Round Iris Panel

A classic stained glass panel with a gorgeous iris design perfect for any window.

Materials

- Iris blue glass
- Green glass
- Clear glass
- U-shaped lead came
- 20-gauge tinned copper wire
- Black patina
- Chain at desired length for hanging

Pattern by Yuliya Brukhanova, Levantese

1. A length of U-shaped lead came will provide support to the perimeter of the Round Iris Panel. To straighten the lead came before using it, secure one end in a vise and pull the piece, holding it with a cloth or towel.

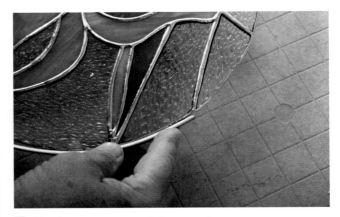

3. Fit the came around the panel.

2. Trim the came with a utility knife.

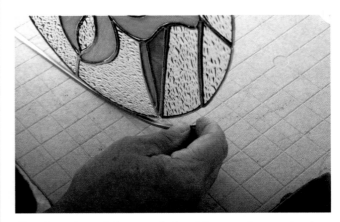

4. The edge of the panel should securely seat in the U-shaped channel.

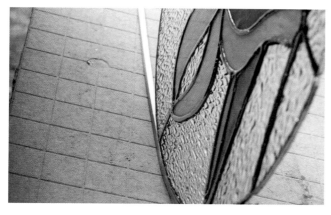

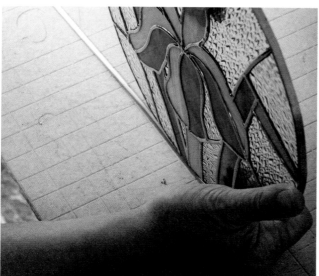

5. Continue around the panel, pressing the came firmly in place.

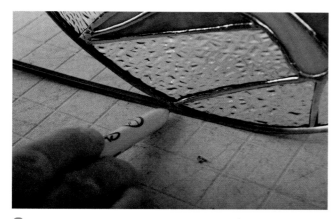

6. Make a mark where the ends of the came meet.

7. Carefully cut at the mark, then pull the ends together as close as possible. Don't worry if they don't quite touch; you can fill in the gap with solder.

8. To work with lead came, you'll use a lower heat setting for the solder. Try 360 degrees.

9. Flux the came joint thoroughly.

10. Solder the ends together. When you work with lead came, you can't let the iron linger too long at one spot. The lead will melt fairly quickly.

11. Solder the entire joint.

TIP Soldering is all about rhythm. Once you get a good tempo going, you'll find that this part of the project can end up being the most enjoyable, though it will take a while to perfect your technique.

12. Flux and solder each point where the came and soldered foil meet.

13. Make a hanger for the panel using 20-gauge wire. Cut a 4- to 5-inch length.

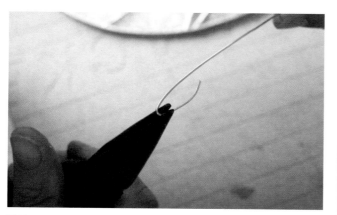

14. Bend it into a long U shape.

15. Slide the wire onto the edge of the panel where one hanger should go—at around 10 o'clock.

16. Make sure the wire touches the soldered seam.

17. Solder the hook to the panel, front and back. Solder a second hook at the top in the same way.

18. Black patina is applied to the solder to darken it. Don't forget to wear rubber gloves when working with patina.

19. When the patina has been applied and rinsed off thoroughly, use window cleaner to make the glass shine.

20. Dry it completely to avoid smudges.

21. The cleaner will bring out the best in the piece.

22. The final step is to attach a chain to the hooks.

23. Use needle-nose pliers to open the end link.

24. Slip the link onto a hook and gently squeeze it shut.

25. Do the other side.

26. Adjust the chain's length as you see fit.

Miniature Glass House

Simple to make, these whimsical houses will liven up any tabletop or mantelpiece.

Materials

- Rich red glass
- Shimmery off-white or silver glass
- Beveled assembly tray
- Small copper tube
- Foam stained glass support blocks
- 20-gauge tinned copper wire
- ⅜-inch-wide copper foil
- Black patina

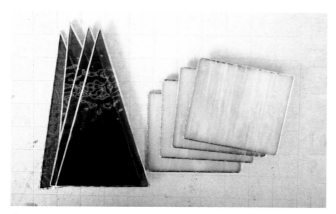

1. Four identical roof triangles and four identical squares will form the house. In general, this is a more complicated project, but the glass-cutting part is pretty easy.

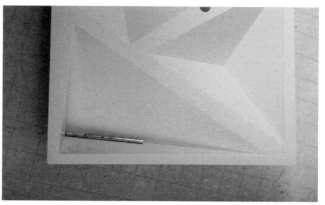

3. Place a piece of copper tubing in the right-angle corner of the tray.

Morton Glass Works
www.mortonglass.com

2. A beveled assembly tray made especially to hold stained-glass projects in place as you solder them is used to put this house together. These trays are available at stained glass shops or online retailers.

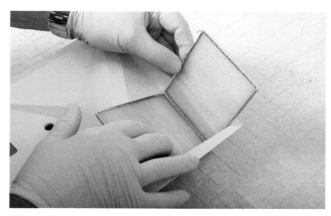

4. Set two square pieces in the right-angle corner of the tray. The edges of the pieces should not overlap but should come together to form a V. The tube will allow you to keep the pieces from overlapping.

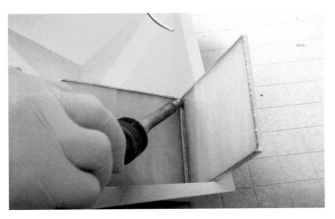

5. Flux and solder the inside seam together by first tacking one side and then the other.

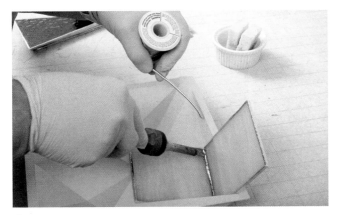

6. Then run a line of solder the length of the seam.

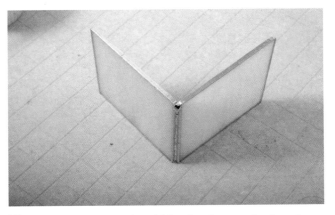

7. The glass pieces should be firmly attached and form a right angle.

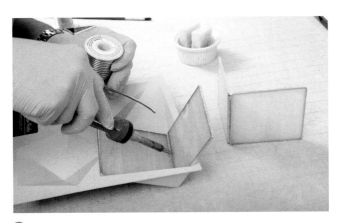

8. Do the same to create another house corner.

9. Set the two corners together so that an unsoldered seam is resting in the tray. Remember to avoid overlapping the edges by using the copper tube. You want them to form a V. This step takes a bit of fiddling to get right.

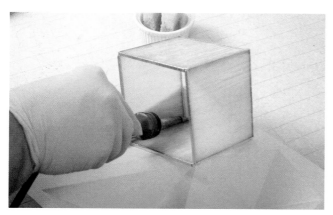

10. Solder the seam together, first tacking the sides then running a line of solder along the whole seam.

11. Gently reposition the house so that the unsoldered seam is in the tray. Solder the seam together.

12. To solder the outside of the house, use foam blocks to support the glass with one seam facing up.

13. Solder the top seam together. You'll find that a generous amount of solder is needed to fill in the gap completely.

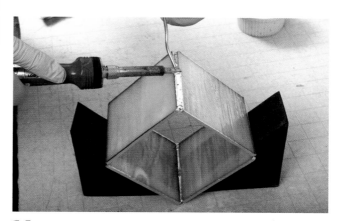

14. Work carefully so the seam is smooth.

TIP Never use anything other than foam blocks especially made for stained glass making. They are flame-resistant. Ordinary foam blocks, as well as wood or cardboard or plastic, can ignite from a splash of hot solder or the touch of a hot iron.

17. The roof is assembled in the same way as the house was. And as with the house, the edges of the roof pieces should not overlap but form a V.

15. Reposition the house to solder the rest of the seams one by one.

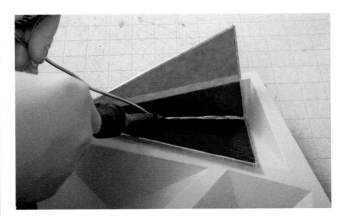

18. Solder two pieces together, then do the two other pieces.

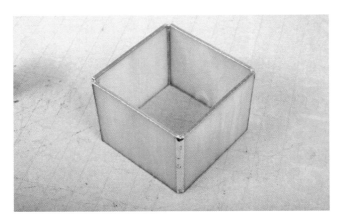

16. The completed house should have four 90-degree corners.

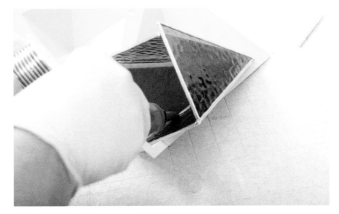

19. Soldering the inside seams to join the two angled sections is a little tricky.

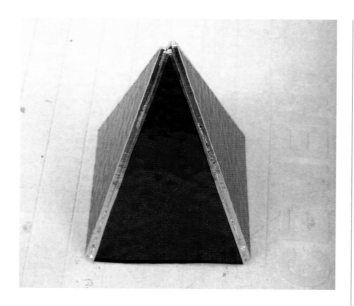

20. When assembled, the roof should sit flat with no wobbling.

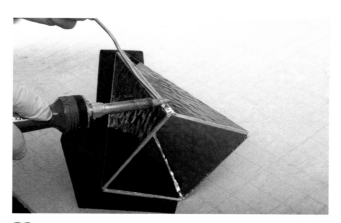

21. Use foam blocks to support the roof to solder the outside seams.

22. Again, you'll use a generous amount of solder.

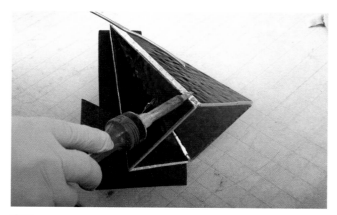

23. Reposition the roof to do the other three sides.

24. The roof should fit the house perfectly.

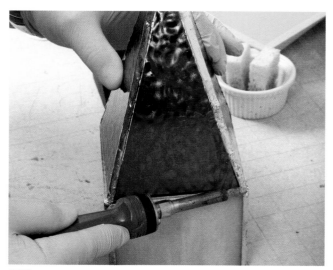

25. To attach roof to house, tack the corners together first.

26. Then run a line of solder the length of the seam. This is easier to do if the house is on its side.

28. Bend a length of 20-gauge tinned copper wire as shown to form the roof peak decoration.

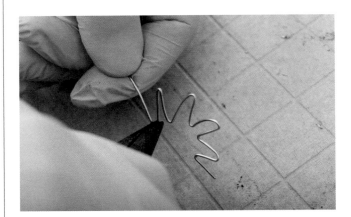

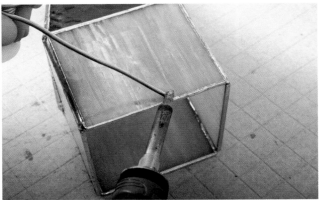

27. Don't forget to tin the bottom edge of the house, front and back.

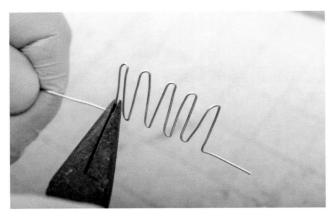

29. Bend bit by bit to form a zigzag pattern.

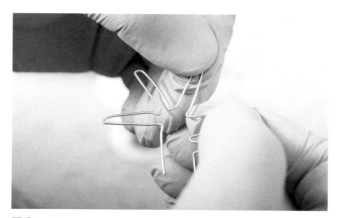

30. The zigzag is then bent to form a starlike pattern.

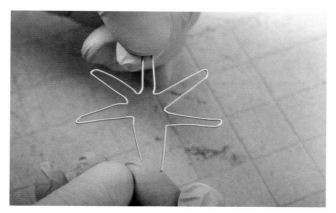

31. Bend the wire by hand to create a shape like this.

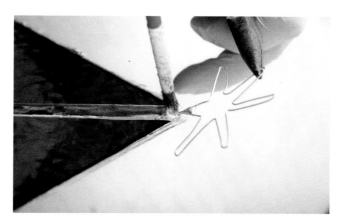

32. Apply flux to both sides of the open section.

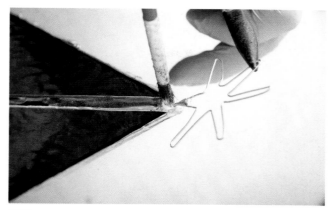

33. Solder the piece to the peak of the roof.

34. Wash and rinse the house thoroughly.

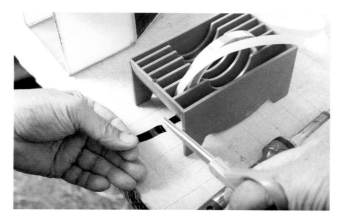

35. Use ⅜-inch-wide foil to create tiny doors and windows.

36. These can be applied to the glass then trimmed. Make sure the glass is dry so the foil will stick.

37. A felt-tip pen is used to sketch out the door's top arch.

38. Little windows in the door are drawn in, too.

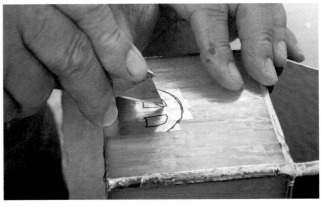

39. Use a sharp craft knife to cut out the windows.

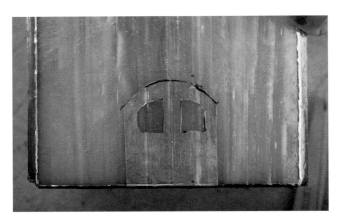

40. Use needle-nose pliers to remove the cut-away foil.

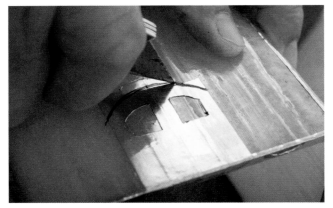

41. A craft or utility knife also is used to cut the door's arch.

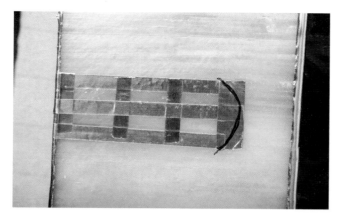

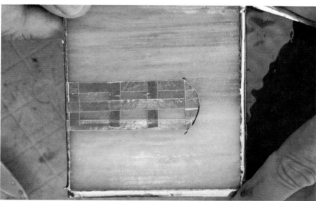

42. Create windows with openings and arched tops using the foil, trimming with a knife.

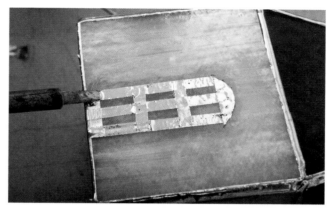

44. Flux the foil then tin the doors and windows.

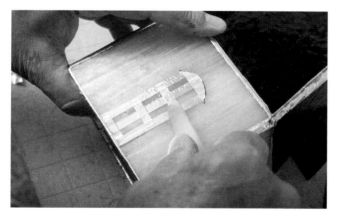

43. Use the fid to smooth the doors and windows and make certain they are firmly adhered to the glass.

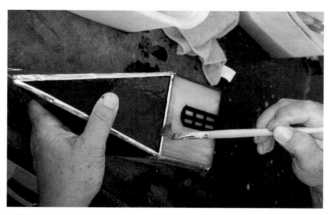

45. A patina is used to darken the foil on the assembled house.

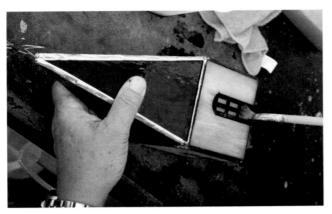

46. Make sure you cover all the foil.

47. Don't forget to apply patina to the wire at the top. As always, wash and rinse the piece thoroughly.

Hinged Jewelry Box

A handmade heirloom to give as a gift or keep for yourself.

Materials

- Shimmering or iridescent glass
- Subtle red shaded glass
- Beveled assembly tray
- Foam stained glass support blocks
- ³⁄₁₆-inch diameter copper tubing
- ³⁄₃₂-inch diameter copper tubing
- 20-gauge tinned copper wire
- Lead came
- Chain for box lid support

1. The glass piece that forms the bottom of the box should have smoothly rounded corners.

2. Use the grinder to smooth off the corners until they are nicely rounded.

3. Foil the glass bottom after grinding.

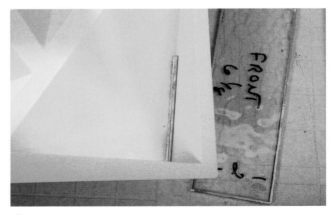

4. Set a piece of tubing into the 90-degree angle of the assembly tray as shown.

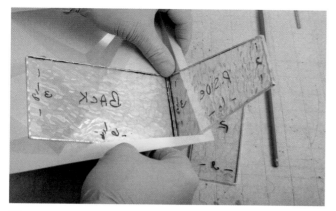

5. Set a side piece in the tray at a right-angle. The edges of the pieces should not overlap but should form an open V on the outside. Setting the vertical piece atop the tubing will help you avoid an overlap.

6. Solder the seam by first tacking each side.

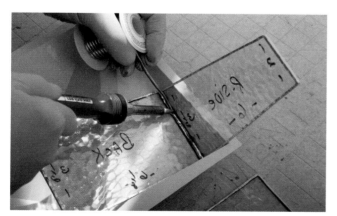

7. Then run a line of solder down the length of the seam.

8. Solder the rest of the pieces together the same way you did for the Miniature House.

9. Foam blocks will support the box frame while you solder the outside edges.

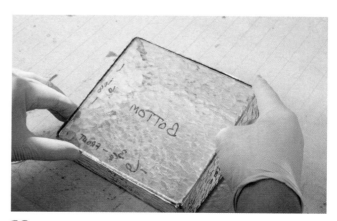

10. When the frame is soldered together, carefully set the bottom piece in place.

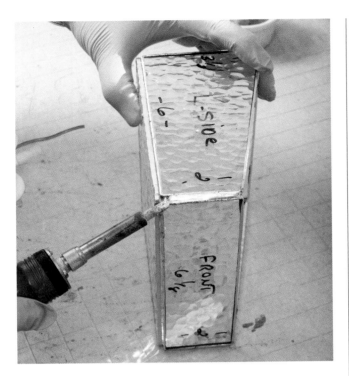

12. Then solder the inside seams.

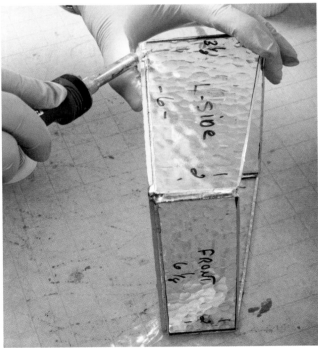

11. Solder the bottom to the frame, tacking the corners together first. Then run a line of solder down each seam.

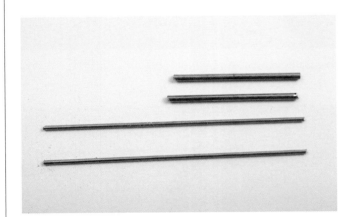

13. When the body of the box is completed, the next step is to create the hinges to attach the lid. Two pieces of copper tubing—one ³/₁₆ inch in diameter, the other ³/₃₂ inch in diameter—are used for this.

14. Lay a length of the thicker tubing along a ruler and mark it at 1¾ inch.

15. Use knife or file edge to make a small nick at the mark.

16. Then break the tube at the nick.

17. Do the same to create another 1¾ length of thicker tubing and two 3-inch lengths of the larger tubing.

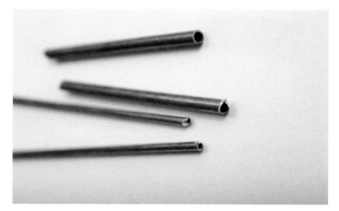

18. The result will be two sets of tubes that will form the hinges.

TIP A drop of oil on the hinges will keep them operating smoothly. But don't apply it until the project is complete, and only use a tiny bit.

21. Next, make an angle in the other side of the inside tube.

19. Insert the smaller tubes inside the larger tubes then use the pliers to bend a slight angle at the end of the inside tube. This will prevent it from sliding down in. Do the same for the second set of tubes.

22. This angle should be 90 degrees.

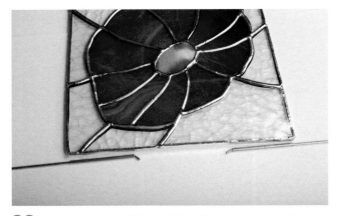

20. The hinges will be soldered to the back edges of the lid, as shown.

23. Do the same for the second hinge.

24. Measure out a length of U-shaped lead came that will run along the back of the lid.

25. Trim the lead came using a sharp craft knife.

TIP The hinge on the box will suffer the most wear and tear. If it comes apart, it is possible to heat up the solder to remove it and replace it with a new one. There's no need to sacrifice the whole box because of a broken hinge.

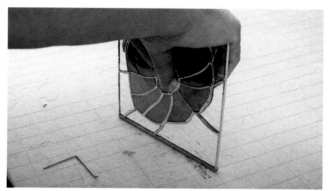

26. Insert the edge of the lid into the channel.

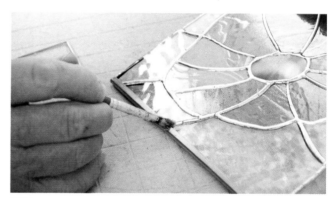

27. Apply flux where the came touches the lid seams.

28. Solder the came at these spots.

29. Set the hinges in place as shown and apply flux. Solder the tube to the lid.

30. Do the same for the second hinge.

31. The hinge should be firmly attached.

32. Set the lid on top of the box body so the inside tubes align with the side corners.

33. To solder the side tubes to the box, support the box with foam blocks so the tube is facing up.

34. Solder the smaller tubes to the box.

35. Solder carefully so you don't prevent the hinge from turning.

36. Do one side, then shift the box to do the other.

37. Be generous with the solder so the tube is firmly attached.

38. The last step is to solder a chain from the lid to the box so it doesn't open too far.

39. Foam blocks will help you support the lid as you solder.

40. Solder one end of the chain to the front bottom corner of the box.

41. Cut the chain to the proper length so that it won't let the lid open much beyond the perpendicular.

PATTERNS

SAND DOLLAR SUNCATCHER

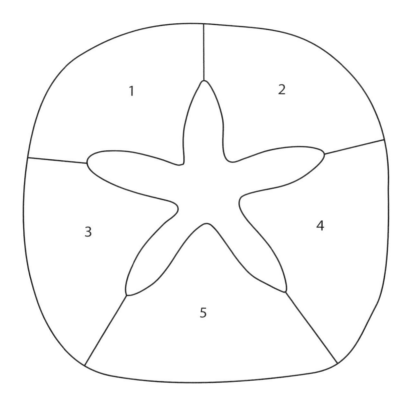

LUCKY SHAMROCK

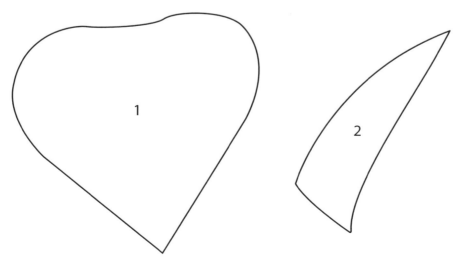

FALLING LEAF

CLASSIC ICICLE ORNAMENT

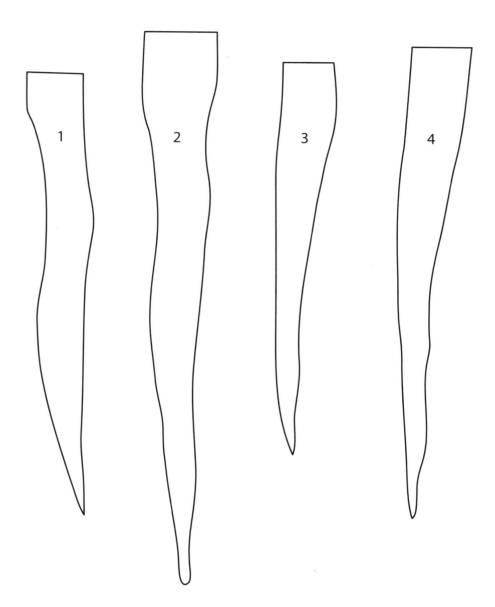

ICICLE ORNAMENT WITH BLING

PAINTED SNOWMAN ORNAMENT

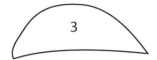

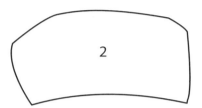

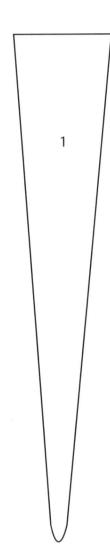

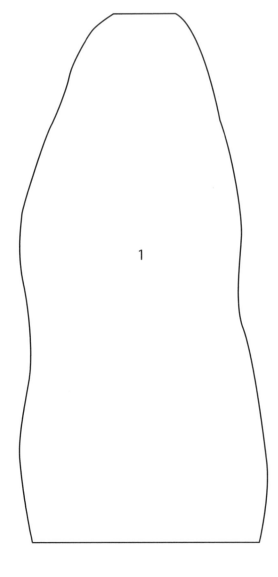

TINY LEAF PENDANT

TINY FEATHER PENDANT

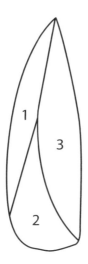

LARGE FEATHER SUNCATCHER

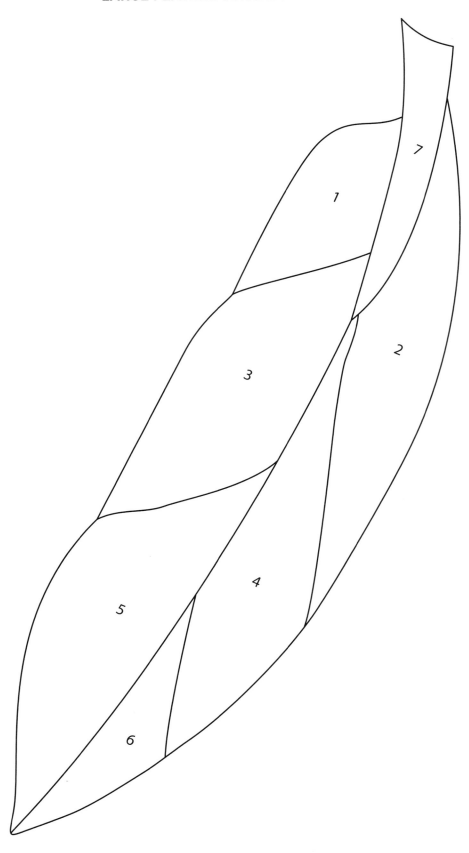

ROUND DECORATED CANDLEHOLDER

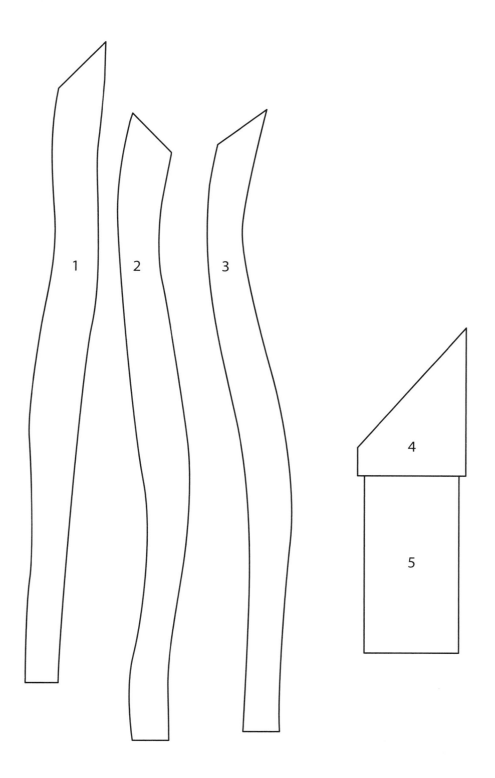

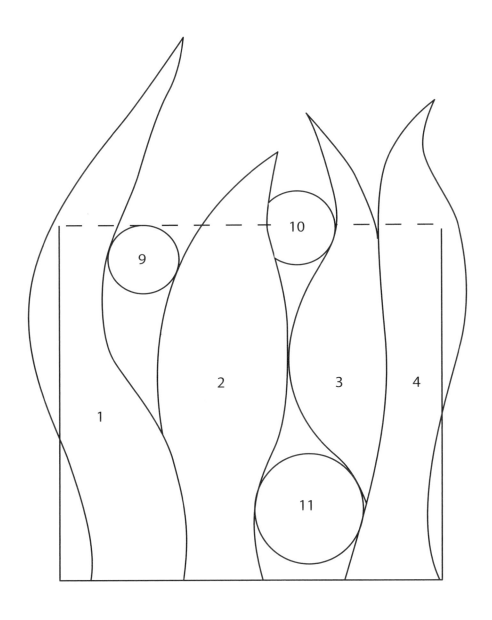

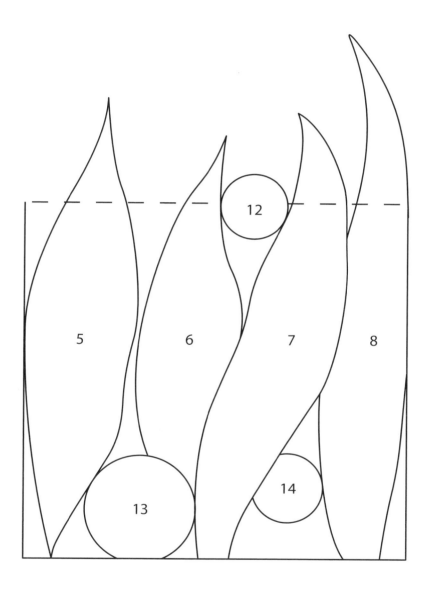

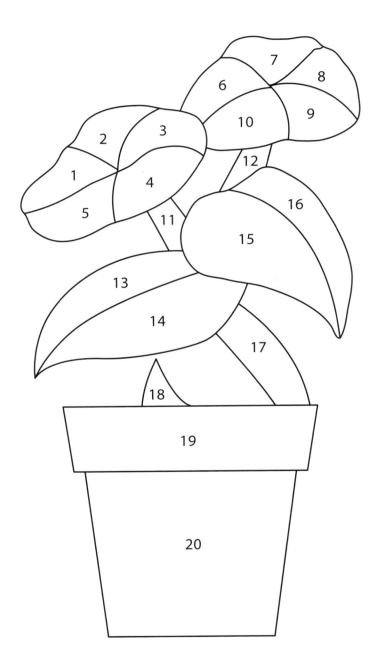

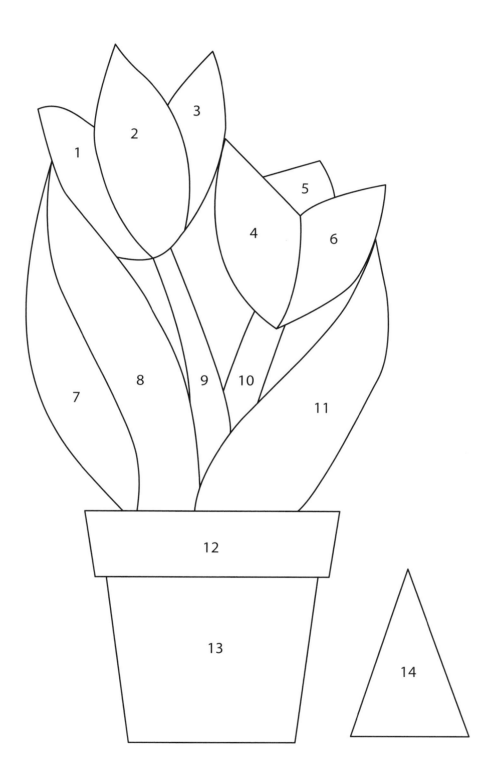

PINEAPPLE NIGHTLIGHT

DRAGONFLY GARDEN STAKE

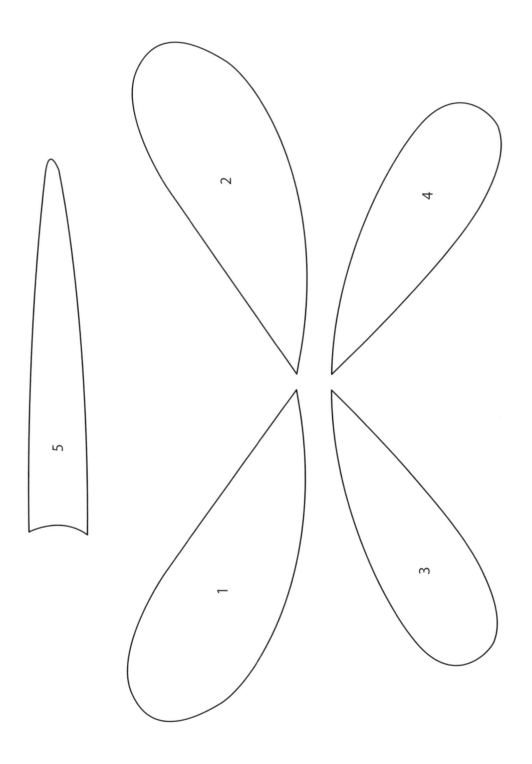

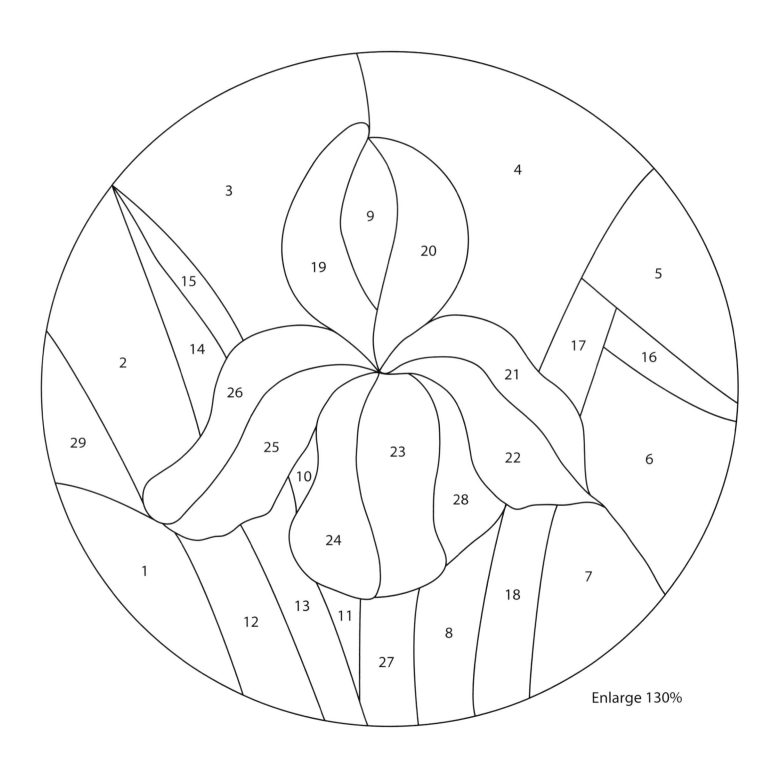

Enlarge 130%

MINIATURE GLASS HOUSE SIDES

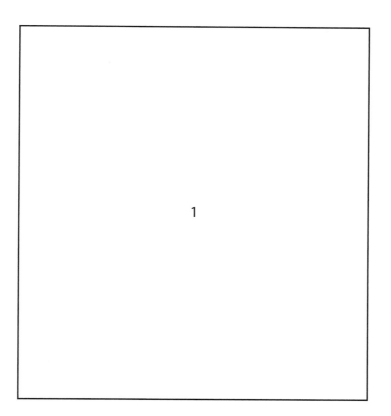

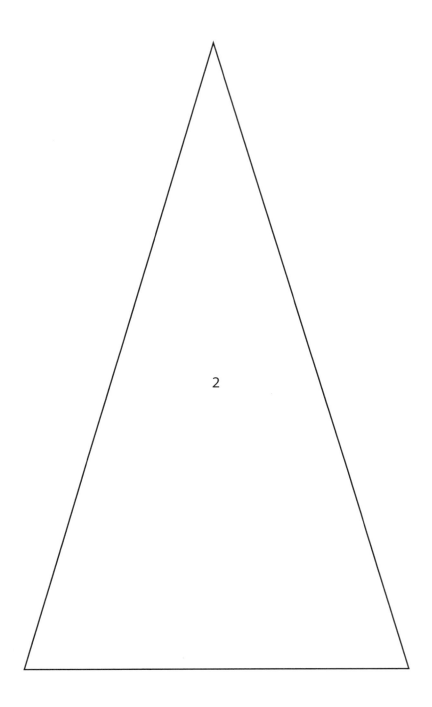

2

HINGED JEWELRY BOX

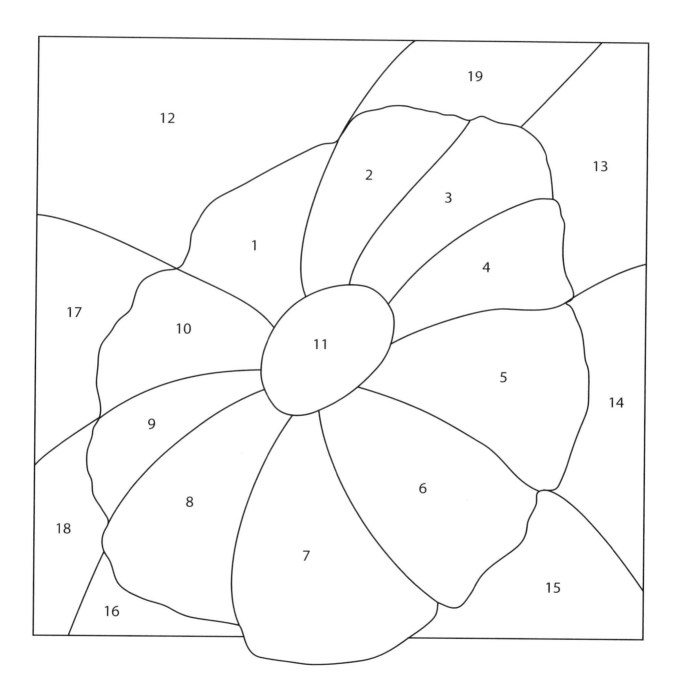

20

HINGED JEWELRY BOX FRONT　　　　**HINGED JEWELRY BOX BACK**

21

22

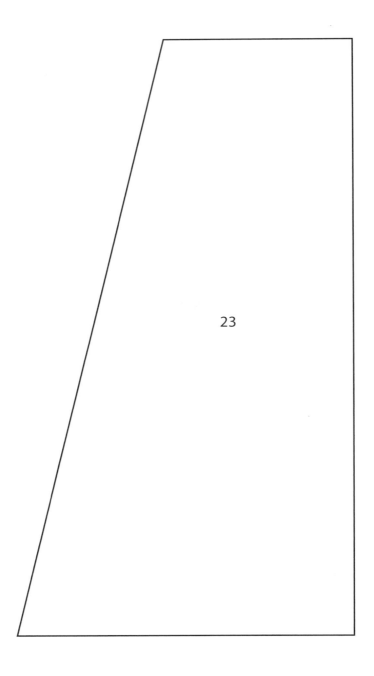

23

OTHER GLASS CRAFT BOOKS
AVAILABLE
FROM STACKPOLE

Basic Glass Fusing

Basic Stained Glass Making

Beyond Basic Stained Glass Making

Decorative Stained Glass Designs

40 Great Glass Fusing Projects

40 Great Stained Glass Projects

Glass Beads

Glass Bead Inspirations

Making Stained Glass Lamps

Stained Glass Painting

Stackpole Stained Glass Patterns

Backyard Birds

Beautiful Leaves

Birds of the Beach

Butterflies and Dragonflies

Garden Flowers

Songbirds

Distributed by
NATIONAL BOOK NETWORK
800-462-6420